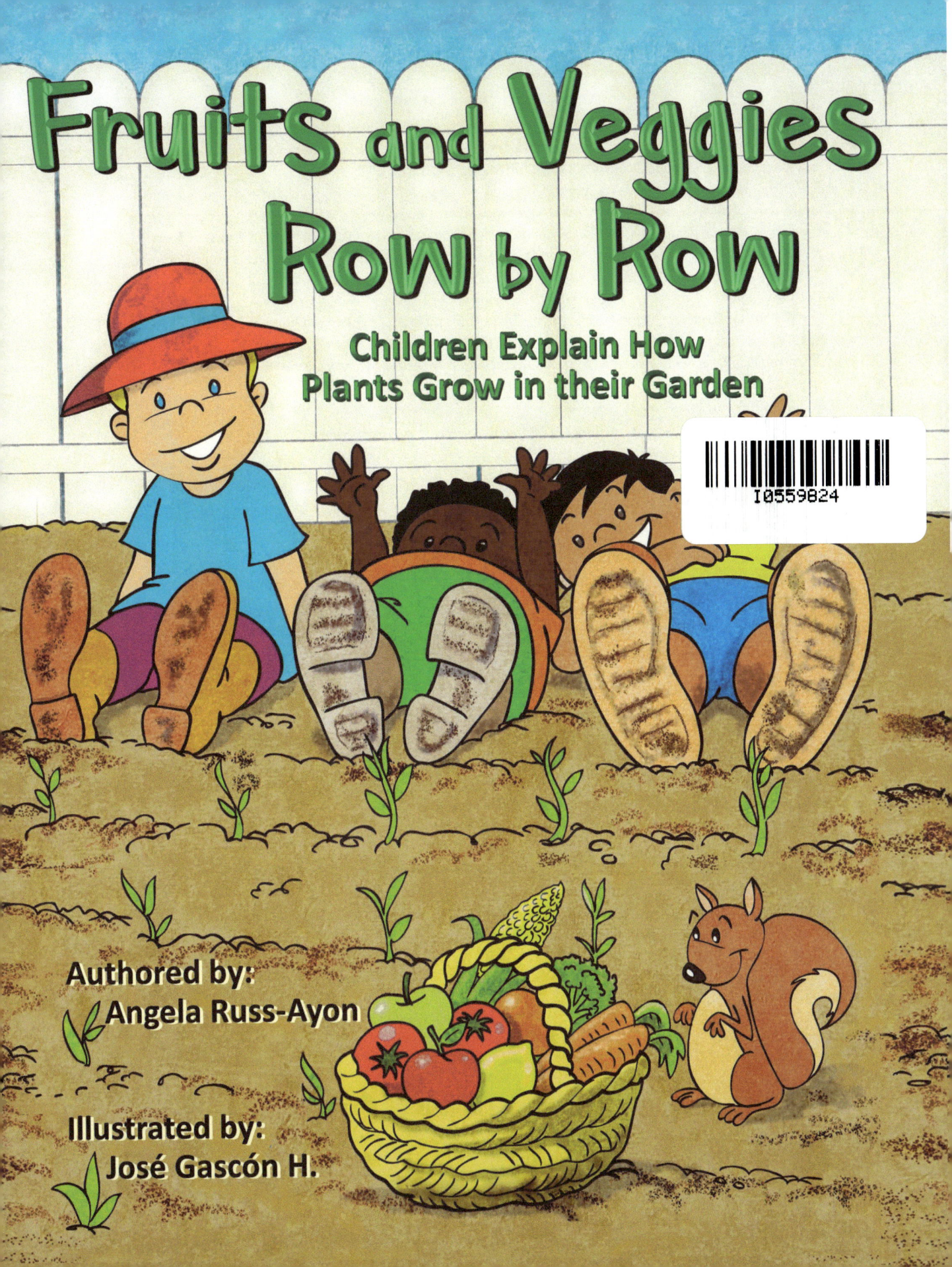

Fruits and Veggies Row by Row

Children Explain How Plants Grow in their Garden

Authored by:
Angela Russ-Ayon

Illustrated by:
José Gascón H.

Other Titles by this Author:

- *Fruits and Veggies Row by Row: Children Explain How Plants Grow in Their Garden* | English
- *Frutas y Vegetales Fila por Fila: Los Niños Explican Cómo Crecen las Plantas en su Jardín* | Spanish & English
- *I Spy Vegetables: A Seek and Find Early Science and Math Experience* | English
- *Espío Vegetales: Una Experiencia Temprana de Ciencias y Matemáticas (Buscar y Encontrar)* | Spanish & English
- *I Spy Fruit: A Seek and Find Early Science and Math Experience* | English
- *Espío Frutas: Una Experiencia Temprana de Ciencias y Matemáticas (Buscar y Encontrar)* | Spanish & English
- *We Eat Food That's Fresh: A Children's Picture Book about Tasting New Fruits and Vegetables (3rd Edition)* | English
- *Comemos Comida Fresca: Un Libro para Los Niños Sobre Probando Nuevas Frutas y Verduras* | Spanish & English
- *Fruits & Veggies Making Faces: A Children's Picture Book About Feelings, Emotions, and Self-Expression* | English
- *We Love the Company: A Children's Picture Book About Table Manners (2nd Edition)* | English
- *Nos Encanta la Compañía: Un Libro Para Niños Sobre Modales en la Mesa* | Spanish & English
- *When You Find Colors and Shapes: A Physically Interactive Early Math and Science-Based Children's Picture Book* | English
- *Cuando Encuentres los Colores y las Formas* | Spanish & English
- *Quand Vous Trouvez les Couleurs et les Formes* | French & English
- *Jisel's Gifts: A Picture Book that Encourages Children to Give Back to the Community* | English

About the Author:

Angela Russ-Ayon resides in Long Beach, California, with her family. She is an author, keynote speaker, producer, and trainer on early childhood development, as well as the owner of the Russ InVision Company children's record label. Her company boasts over $1.5 million in sales, has been presented with nine early childhood music awards of excellence, and is represented by school suppliers nationwide. Her specialty is engaging young children in interactive song and dance using fine and gross motor activities that promote interactive learning, inspire imaginative play, help build brain pathways and bridge educational gaps.

About the Illustrator: José Gascón H.

José Gascón H. holds a degree from The Center of Image and Sound and has worked with former animation directors from major production studios such as Walt Disney, Warner Brothers, Hanna Barbera, and Universal. He spent seven years working as an Art Director and Animation Supervisor for a major corporation in Asia until settling in Toronto, Canada, where he has been serving as adjunct faculty for leading institutions such as The Art Institute, Kennedy College of Technology, and Max The Mutt College of Animation Art & Design. During his extensive career, he has collaborated on popular television shows and feature films.

1st edition
©2018 Russ InVision Company. All rights reserved.
For information about permission to reproduce selections of this book, contact:

Russ InVision

Russ InVision Company
E-mail: info@abridgeclub.com
www.abridgeclub.com

ISBN: 978-1-958627-05-1
IngramSpark ENGLISH Paperback
2nd Edition

We plan to do our gardening
in summer, fall, winter, or spring.
The land is fertile for the tilling,
and our work is so fulfilling.

You can start a garden, too.
Let us show you what to do.
Grab tools like a spade and hoe
to plant your garden row by row.

Follow your design or plan.
Arrange the rows as best you can:
long and straight, side by side,
on a plot, deep and wide.

Scoop in dirt and gently pat
until the mounds are smooth and flat.

Grapes hang clustered all together.
They like warm and cozy weather.

Reach and snip them off a vine.
You have your pile; I have mine.
Use the baskets that we made
to carry grapes into the shade.

Blueberries grow in a batch
over in the berry patch.
From the tiny bell-shaped flowers
comes the fruit with superpowers.

Butterflies feed on them, too,
but there are plenty here for you.
Some are ripe, and some are not.
Do you know which ones I've got?

Move between strawberry rows,
taking short steps on your toes.
Bend down, holding nice and steady.
Pick the red ones. They are ready.

Romaine lettuce takes more room
when the leaves open and bloom.
So does cabbage, but instead,
the center holds a snug, round head.

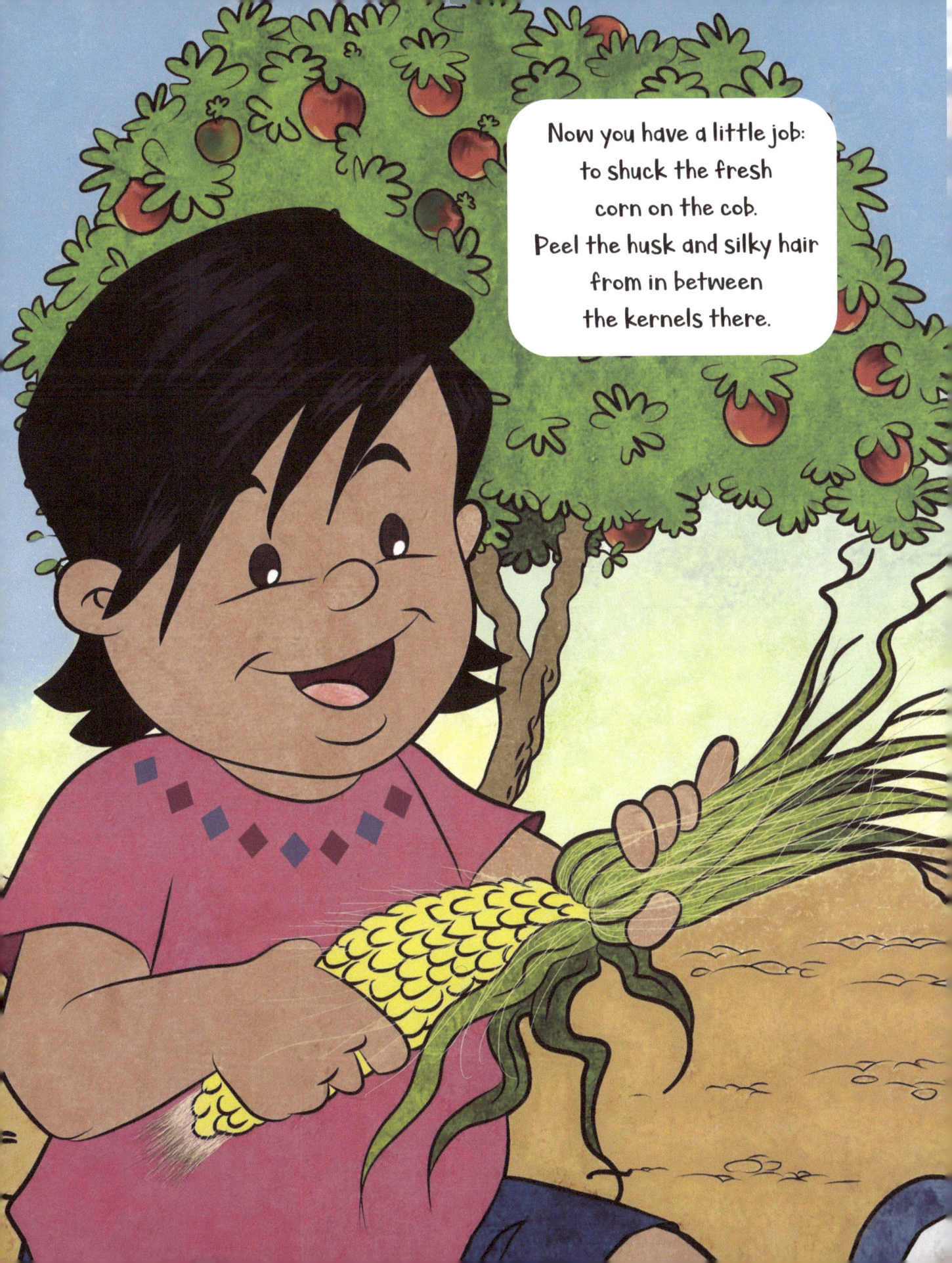

Dig for carrots underground;
that is where the roots are found.
Green stems grow on top, you know,
so look for orange down below.

Pumpkins grow heavy and fat,
with leaves that flip this way and that
on sturdy, swirling, curling vines
that look like twisting wavy lines.

Broccoli buds are green and lumpy.
Their florets feel rough and bumpy.
Cut the firm heads at the top
when you have a hearty crop.

Asparagus shoots out like spears.
New stems will pop up for years,
long and lean, stiff and straight,
with a taste that's worth the wait.

ASPARAGUS

Tomatoes can be large or small:
red, green, yellow... plant them all.
Give each type a roomy pot
resting in a sunny spot.

Bananas hang high in the air.
Tilt your head and look up there.
A yellow peel protects the flavor
of sweet fruit for you to savor.
See them huddled in a bunch?
Who will get them for our lunch?

Branches stretch above the ground
with oranges, juicy and round.
They have segments, pulp, seeds,
and vitamin C your body needs.

Plant the food your family eats,
like cauliflower, squash, or beets -
onions, bok choy, melons, berries,
avocados, peas, or cherries.

Farm your garden row by row
and harvest every crop you sow.

Talking Points and Teachable Moments

- ▲ Plants are living things. Take good care of them.

- ▲ Gardens grow in a variety of places: inside and outside - in pots, raised beds, wall planters, community plots, greenhouses, backyards, and on farms.

- ▲ Identify and classify fruits versus vegetables.

- ▲ The characteristics of fruits and vegetables: color, size, shape, scent, texture, flavor, etc. Use all senses to explore and investigate.

- ▲ Plan and organize a garden:
    - • best season to plant seeds
    - • crops that mature quickly vs. slowly
    - • perfect location for each plant
    - • suitable weather or temperature
    - • variation of plants
    - • edible vs. nonedible plants
    - • managing pests and diseases

- ▲ Gardening tools and equipment: seeds, dirt/soil, shovel, hoe, rake, trowel, bucket, spade, hose, watering can, ladder, ruler, wheelbarrow, pot, basket, trellis, etc.

- ▲ How plants grow differently: roots, vines, bushes, trees, like flowers, at different heights, etc.

- ▲ Plant anatomy - parts/components and function: seed, bulb, leaf, stem, pod, roots, flower bud, branch, ear, rind, trunk, skin, thorns, petals, etc.

- ▲ Edible and nonedible parts of certain plants: stem, leaf, root, skin, flower, pod, pulp, rind, and seeds.

- ▲ Other vocabulary and terminology:
    - • Early math terms: long, straight, deep, wide, high, short, increase, inside, few, big, top, etc.
    - • Gardening terms: dig, plant, water, pour, grow, weed, rock, pebble, patch, plot, ripe, pick, harvest, etc.

- • Movement concepts: pull, dig, drop, pat, walk, twist, peel, hold, tap, catch, tiptoe, stand, stretch, twirl, cut, squeeze, etc.

- ▲ Patterns, lines, and pathways found in and around the garden.

- ▲ The life cycle of fruits and vegetables.

- ▲ The process of photosynthesis: plants make their own food by capturing energy from sunlight and getting their food (nutrients) through natural resources such as the soil, water, and air.

- ▲ Use a magnifying glass to locate the insects and animals on the pages: ladybugs, bees, beetles, butterflies, caterpillars, grasshoppers, snails, worms, ants, spiders, crickets, praying mantises, dragonflies, and stick bugs.

- ▲ The effects of weather on the garden: sunlight, shade, rain, drought, wind, heat, or cold.

- ▲ The scientific method process involves asking a question, guessing, estimating, or predicting (hypotheses), testing with an experiment, analyzing data from the results of the experiment, and drawing a conclusion.

- ▲ Observe, classify, measure, compare, contrast, and question EVERYTHING!

- ▲ Age-appropriate concepts in the life, earth, and physical sciences - botany, biology, and chemistry.

- ▲ Diagram, map, and journal the gardening experience.

www.ingramcontent.com/pod-product-compliance
Lightning Source LLC
Chambersburg PA
CBHW041441120626
46547CB00002B/303